Kim Thompson

TABLE OF CONTENTS

A Pelican Book

Teaching Tips for Caregivers and Teachers:

Research shows that one of the best ways for students to learn a new topic is to read about it.

Before Reading

- Read the title and predict what the book will be about.
- Read the "Words to Know" and discuss the meaning of each word.
- Read the back cover to see what the book is about.

During Reading

- When a student gets to a word that is unknown, ask them to look at the rest of the sentence to find clues to help with the meaning of the unknown word.
- Motivate students with praise and encouragement.

After Reading

- Discuss the main idea of the book.
- Ask students to give one detail that they learned in the book.

Sight Words

a
away
can
eat
find
fly
have
in
jump
little
long
the
what
you

Words to Know

grass

grasshopper

legs

plants

swarms

What can you find in the **grass**?

grass

You can find a little **grasshopper**!

grasshopper

Grasshoppers have long **legs**.

legs

Grasshoppers eat **plants**.

plant

Grasshoppers can fly in **swarms**.

swarm

A grasshopper can
jump away!

Index

Written by: Kim Thompson
Design by: Under the Oaks Media
Series Development: James Earley

Photos: Nico Yoas: cover; irin-k: p. 5; Silvia Dubois: p. 7; Luc Pouliott: p. 9; mchin: p. 11; ProtasovAN: p. 13; Dmytro Khlystun: p. 15

Library of Congress PCN Data
Grasshoppers / Kim Thompson
Bugs in My Yard
ISBN 978-1-63897-428-4(hard cover)
ISBN 978-1-63897-543-4(paperback)
ISBN 978-1-63897-658-5(EPUB)
ISBN 978-1-63897-773-5(eBook)
Library of Congress Control Number: 2021953294
Printed in the United States of America.

Seahorse Publishing Company
www.seahorsepub.com 1-800-387-7650

Published in the United States
Seahorse Publishing
PO Box 771325
Coral Springs, FL 33077

hair

Some hamsters have big **ears**.

ears

Many hamsters have a **cage**.

cage

All hamsters like to run!

INDEX

Written by: Douglas Bender
Design by: Under the Oaks Media
Series Development: James Earley
Editor: Kim Thompson

Photos: Shutterstock: Happy Monkey: cover; Stock Shot: p. 5; Yury Stroykin: p. 7; igorad1: p. 9; Rudmer Zwerver: p. 11; tanya morozz: p. 13; Prakapenka Alena: p. 15

Library of Congress PCN Data
Hamster / Douglas Bender
My First Pet
ISBN 978-1-63897-434-5(hard cover)
ISBN 978-1-63897-549-6(paperback)
ISBN 978-1-63897-664-6(EPUB)
ISBN 978-1-63897-779-7(eBook)
Library of Congress Control Number: 2022932330

Printed in the United States of America.

Seahorse Publishing Company
www.seahorsepub.com

Published in the United States
Seahorse Publishing
PO Box 771325
Coral Springs, FL 33077